MYTHOS ISLAND: CHAPTER 9 — BACK FROM THE BRINK — PART 1

IT'S HARD TO BELIEVE THIS ISLE USED TO BE SO BIG AND BEAUTIFUL!

OR THAT THE CREATURES OF MYTHOLOGY HAVE LIVED HERE FOR MILLENNIA!

THINGS WENT SWELL AS LONG AS MYTHOS THE CARETAKER WAS ABLE TO SEND THEM INTO THE WORLD FROM TIME TO TIME!

SURE! ONE QUICK GLIMPSE OF THESE BEASTIES AND YOU GOTTA BELIEVE THEY'RE REAL!

THAT'S WHAT KEPT THE MYTHS ALIVE! BUT THEN THE GIZMO THAT TRANSPORTED THE CRITTERS GOT BUSTED!

AND THE VERY EXISTENCE OF THIS ISLAND DEPENDS ON THEM BEING SEEN IN OUR WORLD!

GAWRSH! IF WHUT'S LEFT OF THIS ROCKPILE DISAPPEARS IN TH' DRINK, IT'LL BE TH' END OF EARTH'S MYTHS FOREVER!

MYTHS, SHMYTHS! IT'LL BE THE END OF US, TOO!

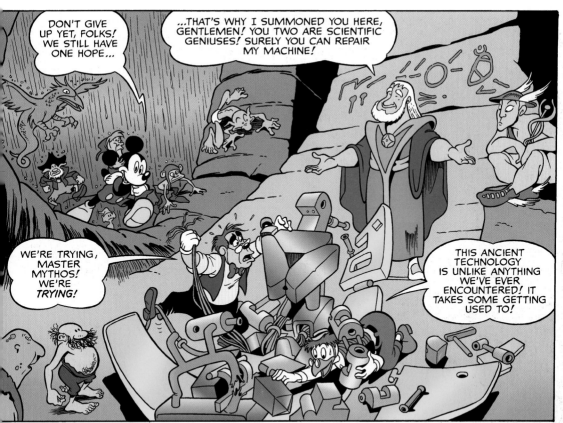

WAIT A MINUTE! YOU SAY FOLKS BACK HOME *SAW* HER? WHY, THAT MUST'VE BEEN RIGHT ABOUT THE SAME TIME GOOFY AND I WERE HERE ON *OUR* FIRST VISIT...

"...AND A PORTION OF THE ISLAND THAT HAD CRUMBLED AWAY MYSTERIOUSLY REAPPEARED RIGHT BEFORE OUR EYES!"

Hmmm! COULD IT *BE?* I WONDER...

MICKEY! IT'S *NO* GOOD! WE CAN'T GET THAT ANTIQUATED MACHINE TO WORK!

WE NEED MORE TIME... BUT THERE *ISN'T* ANY!

IF ONLY WE HAD *OUR* MATTER TRANSPORTERS, WE COULD USE OUR COMBINED BRAIN POWER TO GET THEM TO OPERATE!

WE'RE FAMILIAR WITH OUR *OWN* TECHNOLOGY!

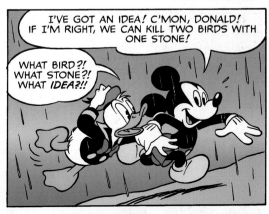

I'VE GOT AN IDEA! C'MON, DONALD! IF I'M RIGHT, WE CAN KILL TWO BIRDS WITH ONE STONE!

WHAT BIRD?! WHAT STONE?! WHAT *IDEA?!!*

WE *KNOW* YOU'RE RELUCTANT, DRAGON! BUT YOU'RE THE ONLY ONE WHO CAN HELP US! PEGASUS IS TOO SMALL FOR THE JOB!

ALL YOUR MYTHOLOGICAL PALS WILL BE SO GRATEFUL! WE WILL BE, TOO! WHAT'A'YA SAY?

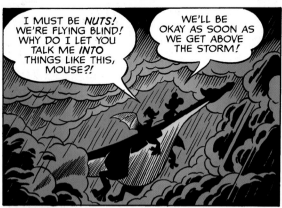

Continued in this issue...

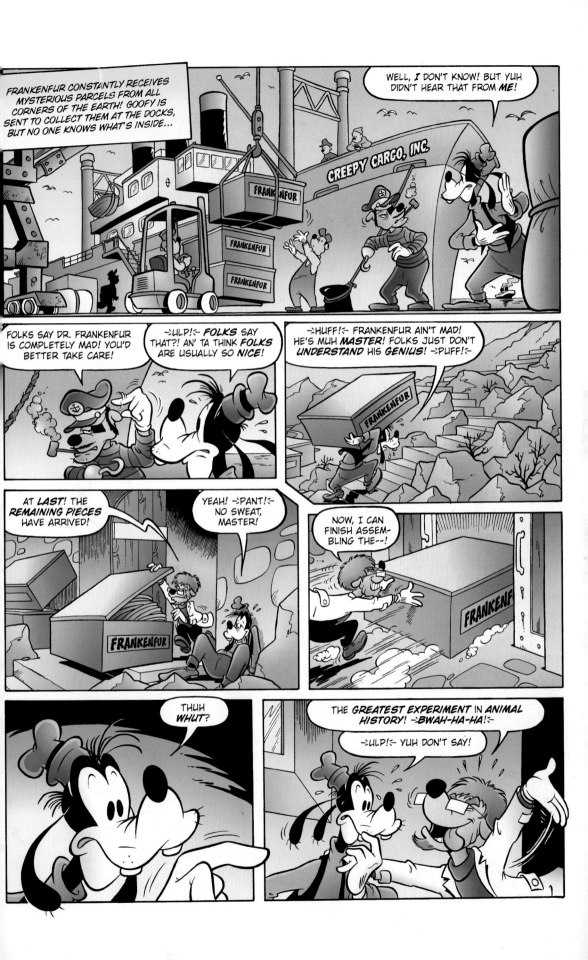

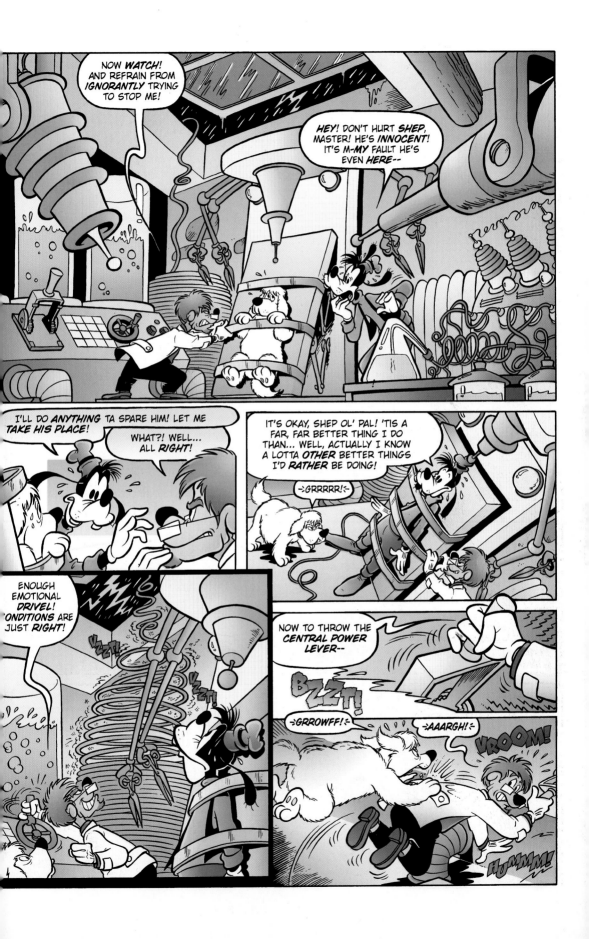

NOW! LET US SEE THE *MIRACLE* MY WILL HAS PERFORMED!

THUH POODLE BRAIN DOESN'T *FEEL* ANY DIFFERENT FROM MINE--

→GAWRSH-A-RING-A-DING-DING!← I'M *HANDSOME!*

YOU'RE A *MASTERPIECE!*

I DON'T GET IT! *THIS* DON'T SEEM SO EVIL!

OF *COURSE* NOT! WHAT COULD HAVE MADE YOU *THINK* ME *EVIL?!*

I'M TIRED OF ONLY SEEING ANIMALS WHEN THEY'RE *SICK!* I WANT TO STOP BEING A *VET* AND MOVE INTO *GROOMING!*

MY AMAZING MACHINES USE SPECIAL *HAIR-RESTORING* RAYS TO *GROW HAIR OUT*, THEN PERFECTLY *GROOM* IT VIA *STATIC ELECTRICITY!*

OF COURSE, IF *OTHER* MOUSETON GROOMERS LEARN OF MY INVENTION BEFORE IT IS READY, THEY MAY *IMITATE* IT!

YOU *KNOW* I MUSTN'T LET CHEAP *MIMICS* BEAT ME INTO ACTION!

GEMSTONE PUBLISHING
presents

© 2005 Disney
Enterprises Inc.

YOUR FAVORITE DISNEY COMICS

Delivered right to your door!

We know how much you enjoy visiting your local comic shop, but wouldn't it be nice to have your favorite
Disney comics delivered to you? Subscribe today and we'll send the latest issues of your favorite comics directly to
your doorstep. And if you would still prefer to browse through the latest in comic art but aren't sure where to go, check
out the Comic Shop Locator Service at www.diamondcomics.com/csls or call 1-888-COMIC-BOOK.

MAIL THIS COUPON TO:
Gemstone Publishing • **P.O. Box 469** • **West Plains, Missouri 65775**

☐ *Walt Disney's Comics & Stories:* $83.40 for 12 issues, 64 pages ($90.00 Canada, payable in US funds) ....$ _____
☐ *Walt Disney's Donald Duck & Friends:* $35.40 for 12 issues, 32 pages ($40.00 Canada, payable in US funds) ....$ _____
☐ *Walt Disney's Uncle Scrooge:* $83.40 for 12 issues, 64 pages ($90.00 Canada, payable in US funds) ....$ _____
☐ *Walt Disney's Mickey Mouse & Friends:* $35.40 for 12 issues, 32 pages ($40.00 Canada, payable in US funds) ....$ _____
☐ *Donald Duck Adventures:* $95.40 for 12 bimonthly issues, 128 pages ($105.00 Canada, payable in US funds) ....$ _____
☐ *Mickey Mouse Adventures:* $95.40 for 12 bimonthly issues, 128 pages ($105.00 Canada, payable in US funds) ....$ _____

SUBTOTAL: $ _____

SALES TAX (MO residents add 6.975% sales tax; MD residents add 5% sales tax): $ _____

TOTAL: $ _____

Name: _____

Address: _____

City: _____ State: _____ Zip: _____

Email: _____

CREDIT CARD:
☐ Visa
☐ MasterCard
☐ Other
_____

Card #: _____

Exp. Date: _____

Walt Disney's
GYRO GEARLOOSE
in
KRANKENSTEIN GYRO

THAT MOVIE WAS SO REAL-LOOKING, IT ALMOST LOOKED *POSSIBLE* TO *BUILD LIFE* FROM MOLECULES!

SEE DOCTOR K BUILD LIVING CREATURE FROM ATOMS! DR. KRANKENSTEIN!

DR. KRANKENSTEIN

THERE ARE ONLY SO MANY ELEMENTS IN LIVING THINGS, AND DR. KRANKENSTEIN FUSED THEM INTO WORKING ORDER WITH BOLTS OF LIGHTNING!

I BET I CAN INVENT A *SIMPLER* WAY TO MAKE LIFE FROM MATTER! .... WHY, OF COURSE!

SELL ME A SUPPLY OF THESE CHEMICALS, WILL YOU, JOHNNY?

CALCIUM, PHOSPHORUS, VITAMINS, LIME, PLASMA, POTASH—

DRUGS

ZINC, SULPHUR, BEEF EXTRACT —! WHAT ARE YOU GOING TO DO, GYRO — MAKE A PIG-FACED, PURPLE *PEOPLE-EATER*?

MAYBE! I'M NOT SURE!

BUT, GOLLY! I *HOPE NOT*!

SOON!

GOT TO BE CAREFUL AND NOT GET TOO MUCH OF ANY *ONE* THING IN THIS MIXTURE!

FUNNY HOW MANY OF THE THINGS THAT MAKE PEOPLE ALSO MAKE PLANTS AND INSECTS AND EVEN POTLIDS!

IT'S JUST A MATTER OF THE WAY THOSE THINGS ARE *PUT TOGETHER*!

I WON'T KNOW *WHAT* I'VE CREATED UNTIL THE MIXTURE TAKES FORM! BUT I THINK IT'LL BE A *BIRD*!

SLUSH
SLUSH

POP

ANYWAY, I MIXED UP THE ELEMENTS THAT ARE FOUND IN *EGGS*! AND I'M PUTTING THEM INTO AN *EGG SHELL* TO *HATCH*!

THERE! *WHATEVER* COMES FROM THIS EXPERIMENT WILL NO DOUBT SURPRISE EVEN *ME*!

I'LL PUT THIS UNDER OLD CLUCKERY CLUCK, WHO HAS BEEN TRYING TO *SET* FOR QUITE A SPELL!

SHE'S DETERMINED TO HATCH *SOMETHING*! IN FACT, SHE'S BEEN TRYING FOR TWO WEEKS TO HATCH A *DOORKNOB*!

HERE, CLUCKERY CLUCK, TRY YOUR SKILL ON *THIS EGG* AND SEE IF YOU DON'T HAVE BETTER LUCK!

CLUCK
CLUCK

THE ICY HAND OF TERROR **GRIPS** THE ENTIRE COUNTRY! THERE SEEMS TO BE NO **RELIEF** FROM THIS STARTLING INFESTATION OF MARAUDING SPIRITS!

H-HELP! OUR TOWN IS FULL OF **GHOSTS!**

THEY'RE **EVERY-WHERE!**

IS THERE **NO ONE** WHO CAN SAVE US FROM THIS TERRIBLE PLAGUE?

D 2003-087

WELCOME ONCE AGAIN TO **"SUPERNATURAL SECRETS"**–THE TV SHOW THAT **DARES** TO PROBE THE FRIGHTENING MYSTERIES OF THE UNKNOWN!

BOY, THIS SHOW SURE IS EXCITING!

PHOOEY! THEY'RE JUST TRYING TO **SCARE** PEOPLE!

SUPERNATURAL PHENOMENA ARE FOUND EVERYWHERE...EVEN IN **DUCKBURG!** AS YOUR FEARLESS HOST, I'M HERE TO INVESTIGATE THESE UNEXPLAINED EVENTS!

WHAT'S TO **EXPLAIN?!** SOME PEOPLE WILL SAY ANYTHING JUST TO GET ON TV!

WITH ME ARE MR. AND MRS. JOHNSON, WHOSE HOUSE IS HAUNTED BY A GHOSTLY PIANO-PLAYER WHO KEEPS THEM UP ALL NIGHT WITH HIS MELODIOUS TUNES!

JOHNSON

IT'S A HORRIBLE GHOST!

HUH?

STOP SCREAMING, LADY! IF THERE *WERE* ANY GHOSTS AROUND, THEY'D BE MORE AFRAID OF *YOU!*

WHAT THE HECK IS *HER* PROBLEM?

YAHHH! IT'S A GHOST!

A G-G-GHOST?

FORGIVE ME, MR. DUCK! I DIDN'T *RECOGNIZE* YOU UNDERNEATH THAT FLOUR!

OKAY, NOW I KNOW WHY THAT SCREAMING MEEMIE WAS SCARED OF ME, BUT, *YOU*, MR. SMITH?

⌐SIGH⌐ IT'S ALL BECAUSE OF THAT SHOW! I'M ASHAMED TO ADMIT IT, BUT "SUPERNATURAL SECRETS" HAS GOTTEN TO *ME*, TOO!

I'M AFRAID IT'S GOING TO BE A WHILE BEFORE PEOPLE GET OVER THIS FOOLISHNESS!

THAT GIVES ME AN *IDEA!* THERE'S AN OPPORTUNITY TO MAKE SOME *BIG* MONEY FROM THIS IDIOCY!

AND SO DONALD STARTS HIS OWN BUSINESS WHERE HE'S THE ONLY EMPLOYEE...

GHOST CHASERS INC.

IT'S TOO BAD THE BOYS ARE OFF AT *CAMP!*

THEN HE TAKES OUT ADS IN THE DUCKBURG NEWSPAPER...

LISTEN TO THIS! "DO YOU SUFFER FROM A SURPLUS OF SCARY SPIRITS? ARE YOU UNNERVED BY THE UNNATURAL! IF THAT'S THE CASE... CALL *GHOST CHASERS!* OUR TRAINED PROFESSIONALS BOOT ANY AND ALL SUPERNATURAL SPOOKIES STRAIGHT BACK TO THE OTHER SIDE!"

...ON THE RADIO...

GOT EXCESS ECTOPLASM? LET *GHOST CHASERS* RINSE THEM OUT OF YOUR HAIR!

...AND ON TELEVISION!

WHEN THE SPOOKS SCARE YOU, WE SCARE *THEM* RIGHT BACK...*AND AWAY!*

LATER...

HA! THIS IS THE *BEST* IDEA I'VE EVER HAD! BUSINESS IS BOOMING! HERE COMES *ANOTHER* CALL!

A HAUNTING AT 11203 PEONY AVENUE? I'M ON MY *WAY!*

I'M SO FRIGHTENED! THERE SIMPLY *MUST* BE A GHOST IN MY HOUSE! EVERY CAKE I'VE BAKED IN THE LAST WEEK HAS *VANISHED* DURING THE NIGHT!

NO NEED TO WORRY, MRS. MARTIN! JUST BAKE ANOTHER CAKE! WHILE YOU'RE ASLEEP TONIGHT, I'LL STAND GUARD IN YOUR HOUSE–BUT DON'T TELL *ANYONE* I'M HERE!

THAT NIGHT, A FURTIVE FIGURE SLIPS INTO THE KITCHEN...

A-HA! PUT IT DOWN, YOU... HEY, WHO *ARE* YOU?

I'M *MR.* MARTIN!

BUT *WHY* ARE YOU...?

PLEASE...I'VE BEEN EATING MY SWEETIE'S AWFUL CAKES FOR *YEARS!* I JUST COULDN'T EAT ANOTHER BITE! SO I'VE BEEN GETTING RID OF THEM WHEN I COME HOME FROM *WORK* EVERY NIGHT!

IF YOU PROMISE TO STOP THROWING THE CAKES OUT, I WON'T TELL YOUR WIFE! AND SHE'LL BE HAPPY I SOLVED HER PROBLEM!

ALL RIGHT, I PROMISE!

AND SO...

WELL, MRS. MARTIN, YOUR WORRIES ARE OVER! THAT'S ONE GHOST WHO WON'T BE COMING BACK! AND HERE'S THE BILL!

OH, DEAR! IT WOULD HAVE BEEN CHEAPER TO *KEEP* THE GHOST!

THE NEXT DAY, IN ANOTHER HOUSE...

I'M AT THE END OF MY ROPE! WHEN I'M WORKING ON MY COLLECTION, THAT BROKEN OLD *FAN* WILL START UP BY ITSELF!

THAT'S STRANGE!

RRRR!

THERE IT GOES NOW! SOME MALICIOUS GHOST MUST BE TURNING IT ON SO MY STAMPS WILL ALL BLOW AWAY!

HMM! I NOTICED THAT THE FAN CAME ON WHEN THE MAN'S *DOG* WALKED ACROSS THE CARPET! THAT *CAN'T* BE A COINCIDENCE!

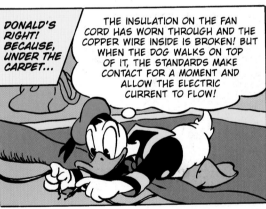

DONALD'S RIGHT! BECAUSE, UNDER THE CARPET...

THE INSULATION ON THE FAN CORD HAS WORN THROUGH AND THE COPPER WIRE INSIDE IS BROKEN! BUT WHEN THE DOG WALKS ON TOP OF IT, THE STANDARDS MAKE CONTACT FOR A MOMENT AND ALLOW THE ELECTRIC CURRENT TO FLOW!

AND THE FAN SWITCH HAS BEEN LEFT IN THE *"ON"* POSITION!

WHEN THE CUSTOMER ISN'T LOOKING, DONALD SPLICES THE WIRE, FIXING THE PROBLEM...

GOOD NEWS! NOT *ONLY* DID I TAKE CARE OF THAT ANNOYING GHOST FOR YOU, I *ALSO* REPAIRED YOUR FAN! HERE'S THE BILL!

YEOW!

NEW CUSTOMERS KEEP CALLING! THE NEXT DAY...

WE'RE TERRIFIED BECAUSE WE HEAR *CHAINS* RATTLING ALL NIGHT LONG UP IN THE ATTIC!

JUST LEAVE THAT PESKY POLTERGEIST TO ME!

INSPECTING THE ATTIC, DONALD SEES PIGEONS FLY IN THROUGH A HOLE AT NIGHT TO ROOST...

I GET IT! THE PIGEONS FLY AROUND THE ATTIC IN THE DARK AND RUN INTO THOSE OLD CHAINS HANGING THERE!

SO I'LL PLUG UP THE *HOLE*...

...AND TAKE THE CHAINS DOWN!

CHALK UP ANOTHER *ECTOPLASM EVICTION*, FOLKS! YOUR GHOSTS HAVE GONE. FEEL FREE TO ADD A *GENEROUS* TIP TO THIS BILL!

AAARGH!

THE FOLLOWING DAY...

I'VE BEEN AFRAID TO GO UP IN THE ATTIC EVER SINCE I BOUGHT THIS HOUSE A MONTH AGO!

WHENEVER I OPEN THE ATTIC DOOR, I SEE A HORRIBLE *MONSTER*!

NOT TO WORRY, MA'AM! THAT MONSTER IS AS GOOD AS GONE!

SOON, IN THE ATTIC...

SO *THAT'S* HER MONSTER! THIS MIRROR IS RIGHT IN FRONT OF THE DOORWAY...

THE LADY IS REALLY JUST SEEING HER OWN *REFLECTION*!

I'LL SOLVE THE PROBLEM BY MOVING THE MIRROR SO SHE CAN'T SEE IT WHEN SHE COMES IN!

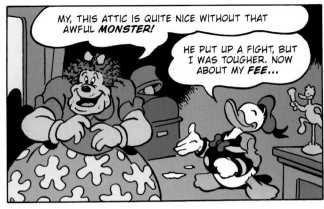

MY, THIS ATTIC IS QUITE NICE WITHOUT THAT AWFUL *MONSTER!*

HE PUT UP A FIGHT, BUT I WAS TOUGHER. NOW ABOUT MY *FEE...*

THE NEXT DAY, DONALD GETS A CALL FROM SOME PEOPLE WHO LIVE NEAR A DESERTED OLD HOUSE...

THERE'S A GHOST HAUNTING THAT HOUSE AND IT'S SCARING US OUT OF OUR WITS!

IT'S *AWFUL!* IT KEEPS US AWAKE ALL NIGHT WITH WEIRD LIGHTS AND LOUD NOISES!

HMM...THIS MAY BE A LEVEL FIVE HAUNTING!

PLEASE! YOU'VE *GOT* TO HELP US!

OUR NERVES ARE SHOT AND WE CAN'T AFFORD TO MOVE FROM HERE!

I'LL TAKE CARE OF THIS, FOLKS...AND I'LL EVEN KNOCK 10% OFF MY BILL!

HMMM! I SEE A REAL-ESTATE DEVELOPMENT COMPANY OWNS THIS HOUSE! THAT MAKES ME *SUSPICIOUS!*

THAT NIGHT, DONALD WAITS ALONE IN THE HOUSE TO SEE WHAT HAPPENS...

I'LL BET THAT REAL-ESTATE COMPANY IS TRYING TO SCARE THE FOLKS WHO LIVE AROUND HERE INTO SELLING THEIR HOMES DIRT *CHEAP!*

THEN IT CAN BUY UP THE WHOLE NEIGHBORHOOD, TEAR DOWN ALL THE HOUSES, AND MAKE A FAT *PROFIT* PUTTING UP CONDOS, COUNTRY CLUBS, AND EXPENSIVE COFFEE SHOPS!

IT'S A CRAFTY SCHEME, BUT I SPOTTED IT A *MILE* AWAY!

CREAK! CREAK!

SOMEONE'S COMING!

NOW I'LL SEE WHO'S TRYING TO SPOOK THE NEIGHBORS WITH SPURIOUS SPIRITS!

OKAY, PAL! YOUR GAME IS OVER! I CAN SEE RIGHT *THROUGH* YOU AND— HUH?!

OOF!

BONK!

AREN'T YOU BEING A LITTLE *RUDE*? WE HAVEN'T EVEN BEEN PROPERLY INTRODUCED YET!

GASP! THIS IS IMPOSSIBLE! I REALLY *CAN* SEE RIGHT THROUGH YOU!

THAT SORT OF GOES WITH MY BEING A *GHOST* AND ALL! NOW WHO ARE *YOU*?

AH, I'M DONALD DUCK FROM THE GHOST CHASERS AGENCY AND...

...AND I'M HERE TO TOSS YOU *OUT* OF HERE! NOW HIT THE BRICKS! BEAT IT! SCRAM!

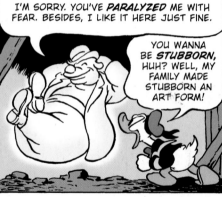

I'M SORRY. YOU'VE *PARALYZED* ME WITH FEAR. BESIDES, I LIKE IT HERE JUST FINE.

YOU WANNA BE *STUBBORN*, HUH? WELL, MY FAMILY MADE STUBBORN AN ART FORM!

SO MUCH FOR MY *LOGICAL* EXPLANATIONS! NOW I HAVE TO FIGURE OUT HOW I'M GONNA GET RID OF A *REAL* GHOST!

THE FOLLOWING NIGHTS, DONALD TRIES TO DRIVE THE GHOST OUT BY SMASHING UP THE HOUSE...

THE HOUSE IS FALLING *DOWN!* RUN FOR YOUR.. AH...*LIFE!*

THEN HE TRIES INSULTING HIM...

HA! HA! HA! YOU'RE THE GOOFIEST-LOOKING GHOST I'VE EVER SEEN! THE ONLY THING SCARY ABOUT *YOU* IS THAT I MIGHT LAUGH MYSELF SICK! *HO! HO!*

AND THEN SCARING HIM...

BOOOOO!

BUT NOTHING WORKS!

—>GROAN!<—

I'M NOT GOING, KID! WATCHING YOU WORK IS MORE FUN THAN THAT TV SHOW!

THE MEDIA CATCHES WIND OF DONALD'S FAILURE...

EXTRA! EXTRA! READ ALL ABOUT IT! GHOST CHASER'S FRIGHTENING FLOP!

AND SOON...

GHOST CHASERS INC.

GROAN! THIS BUSINESS IS TANKING! NOBODY'S CALLING EXCEPT FOR THE BILL-COLLECTORS! IF I DON'T GET SOME JOBS, I'LL BE BUST IN A *WEEK!*

HMM! THE SIGN ON THAT TRUCK JUST GAVE ME AN IDEA! I'LL TALK TO THE GHOST ABOUT IT TONIGHT!

MOVERS

7516

THAT NIGHT...

BE A SPORT! LEAVE *THIS* HOUSE AND I'LL SET YOU UP IN *ANOTHER* ONE!

WELL, I DON'T KNOW...

IT'S TOO BAD ARTHUR QUIT ON ME LIKE THAT! THAT GHOST WAS A GOOD PARTNER AND BROUGHT IN A LOT OF BUSINESS— AND I DIDN'T EVEN HAVE TO *PAY* HIM!

WHAT THE?! THE BOYS MUST HAVE GOTTEN BACK FROM CAMP EARLY AND THROWN A PARTY FOR THEIR PALS! I'LL PUT AN END TO *THIS!*

YOU BOYS KNOW BETTER THAN TO DISTURB OUR *NEIGHBORS* THIS WAY! I'M GOING TO GROUND YOU FOR A *MONTH!*

WHERE ARE YOU HIDING? COME OUT!

I'M OVER *HERE*, DONALD!

ARTHUR?! I'M SO GLAD TO SEE YOU!

ME, TOO!

KA-CHING! I'VE A FEELING MY BUSINESS IS ABOUT TO START *BOOMING* AGAIN!

TELL ME, ARTHUR...WHY DID YOU LEAVE THAT HOUSE BEFORE I COULD PRETEND TO CHASE YOU OUT?

DONALD, OLD CHUM, I WAS GETTING *TIRED* OF MOVING ALL THE TIME! SO I MOVED INTO *THIS* HOUSE! I LIKE IT SO MUCH THAT I'VE DECIDED TO STAY FOR A LONG *LONG* TIME!

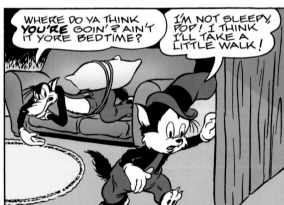

AND I'M **DEPENDING** ON YOU TO SEE THAT HE ALWAYS DOES THE RIGHT THING, JIMINY!

SLAP!

IN THE TWINKLING OF AN EYE, THE FAIRY DISAPPEARS...

YOU **CAN'T** DO THIS TO ME!

TOO LATE! SHE'S GONE! ONLY THE STAR'S LEFT!

WELL! LEAD ON! WHERE **IS** YOUR FATHER?

FOLLOW ME, SIR! I THINK HE'S HOME!

IMAGINE **ME!** THE CONSCIENCE OF THE **BIG BAD WOLF!** IT'S THE TOUGHEST JOB OF MY WHOLE CAREER!

MORNING...

OF ALL TH' COLOSSAL NERVE... A **CRICKET**... IN **BED** WITH ME!

CHIRP... CHIRP!

GIT OUTA MY HOUSE, AN' **STAY GITTED**, YOU CHIP OFF AN OLD CHIRP!

WHY, JIMINY... I DIDN'T EXPECT TO SEE YOU UP SO EARLY!

IT WAS YOUR FATHER'S IDEA, I ASSURE YOU! HE **THREW** ME OUT!

THEN YOU'D BETTER GET RIGHT BACK, 'CAUSE IT'S **YOUR DUTY** TO STAY RIGHT WITH HIM TO KEEP HIM OUT OF **MISCHIEF!**

LEAVING THEIR FRIENDS BEHIND ON THE RAPIDLY DISINTEGRATING MYTHOS ISLAND, MICKEY AND DONALD ENLIST THE AID OF A RELUCTANT DRAGON TO EMBARK ON A DARING RESCUE MISSION...

YOU AND YOUR BIG IDEAS, MOUSE! BARELY UNDERWAY AND ALREADY WE'RE ABOUT TO GET *CREAMED* BY A JUMBO JET!!

KEEP YOUR SHIRT ON, DONALD! THIS BIG BEASTIE IS NIMBLE ENOUGH TO AVOID A MID-AIR COLLISION! SEE?!

D 2002-266

LOOK! LOOK! THERE'S A FLYING *MONSTER* OUT THERE!

HAH! GET A LOAD OF THE RUBBER-NECKERS! THEY'VE NEVER *SEEN* A REAL LIVE DRAGON BEFORE!

AT THAT MOMENT, ON MYTHOS ISLAND...

≈GASP!≈ NOT AN HOUR AGO, I WATCHED THAT CLIFF CRUMBLE AWAY!

BUT NOW IT'S *RE-MATERIALIZING* OUT OF THIN AIR! WHAT GIVES?!

SHORTLY...

MASTER MYTHOS, WE CAN SOLVE OUR PROBLEMS BY LINKING OUR TWO MACHINES TOGETHER THUS ELIMINATING MOST PREVIOUS ERRORS!

BUT TO MAKE SURE THEY REALLY WORK CORRECTLY, WE NEED TO LAY OUR HANDS ON...

...AN OBJECT WITH *FLAWLESS* CRYSTAL STRUCTURE!

HUH?!!

BUT... BUT... MY *DIAMOND*... IT'S THE *ONLY* THING OF VALUE I'VE FOUND ON THIS ISLAND... YOU... YOU WANT ME TO...??

NO! NO! *NEVER!* I *WON'T* LET YOU HAVE IT!

SORRY, SCROOGY! IT'S FER TH' GOOD O' TH' GROUP!

HUURFF!!

SNATCH!!

SIGH! I SUPPOSE AFTER THE INITIAL SHOCK WORE OFF, I'D HAVE COME AROUND AND GIVEN UP THAT STONE!

GOSH, UNCA SCROOGE! YOU'RE A REGULAR *HERO!*

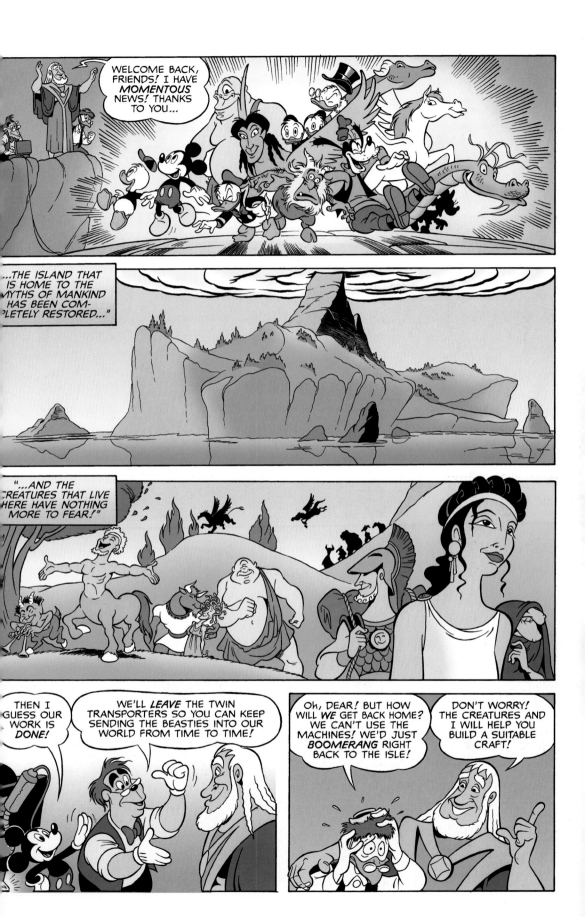

The End

YEAH? WELL THE WAY HE ACTED YOU'D THINK HIS DOGGONED DERBY WAS LINED WITH **DIAMONDS!**

MIDNIGHT, AND NEFARIOUS DOINGS ARE UNDER WAY IN THE GILTBUNDLE MANSION!

HOW LONG WERE YOU A BUTLER IN THIS JOINT, LEROY?

ONLY LONG ENOUGH TO INSURE THE SUCCESS OF OUR LITTLE VENTURE, DIPPY!

I'LL SAY! A KEY TO THE HOUSE, THE ALARM CODE AND THE COMBINATION TO THE SAFE! YOU **DO** HAVE THE COMBINATION, DON'T YA?

MOST ASSUREDLY! IT'S WRITTEN ON THE LINING OF MY HAT! JUST A QUICK—

YE GADS! THIS ISN'T MY HAT!

WHATTAYA MEAN IT AIN'T YER HAT? YOU USUALLY GO AROUND WEARIN' OTHER PEOPLE'S HATS?

OF COURSE NOT! I— GOOD GRIEF! THE **OLD DUCK!** OF **COURSE!**

WHAT OLD DUCK? WHATTAYA TALKIN' ABOUT?

LEROY EXPLAINS—

CRIMINEY! A FORTUNE IN JEWELRY AT OUR FINGER TIPS AND YOU GOTTA GO AN' LOSE YER HAT!

WHICH MEANS WE HAVE NO CHOICE!

WE MUST LOCATE THAT OLD DUCK AND GET MY HAT BACK!

OH, SIMPLE-DIMPLE! THERE'S A LOT OF OLD DUCKS IN THIS BURG!

YES, BUT I DOUBT VERY MANY OF THEM ARE NAMED **"McFOWL"**! SEE?

LET'S GO FIND A PHONE BOOK!

RUMPUS McFOWL

MORNING COMES, AND FOR UNCLE RUMPUS, CONFUSION!

WELL, I'LL BE BLESSED! THIS ISN'T MY HAT! LOOK WHAT'S WRITTEN ON THE LINING! "12-18-61"!

HMM! SOUNDS TO ME LIKE THE COMBINATION TO A **SAFE**! OR SOMEBODY'S BIRTH DATE!

THE GUY I BUMPED INTO YESTERDAY GOT **MY** HAT! HOW ON EARTH AM I EVER GOING TO **FIND** HIM?

MAYBE YOU'LL GET LUCKY!

MEANWHILE—

WHOA! McFOWL'S ADDRESS IS SCROOGE McDUCK'S **MONEY BIN**!

DOWN BOY! STOP DROOLING!

KEEP OUT!

SCRAM

YA GOTTA ADMIT THIS MAKES A PILE OF JEWELRY LOOK LIKE SMALL POTATOES!

MAYBE SO! BUT WE'D NEVER BE ABLE TO PULL OFF A CAPER OF THAT MAGNITUDE! BESIDES— AH, **LOOK**!

THERE HE IS! AND I BET THAT'S **MY** HAT HE'S WEARING!

LET'S **NAIL** HIM!

EASY, DIPPY! WE'LL JUST ASK **NICELY**! HE'LL NO DOUBT BE HAPPY TO GET HIS OWN HAT BACK!

RUMPUS IS MORE THAN MERELY HAPPY! HE IS **RHAPSODIC**!

AH, MY BELOVED **HAT**! MY OWN NOBLE LID AT LAST! THE BALM TO MY SCONCE LO, THESE MANY YEARS!

WHAT A MADHOUSE DUCKBURG IS TODAY!

ONE WONDERS HOW MUCH WORSE IT CAN GET?

IT'S A GOOD THING **OUR** DERBYS DON'T FIT! OTHERWISE THEY'D BE LONG GONE!

HEY! HERE COMES THAT GUY WE RAN INTO YESTERDAY!

HE AND HIS PAL SURE LOOK **DESPERATE**!

IT AIN'T **NONE** OF THESE, LEROY!

NOR THESE!

L A T E R . . .

HEY! **THERE'S** ONE WE MISSED!

DIPPY, **WAIT**!

THAT'S A WOODEN **CARVING**, YOU IDIOT! TRY TO BE **PRODUCTIVE**, WILL YOU?

Y' SHOULDA WRITTEN THE COMBINATION ON YER **FOREHEAD**, LEROY! **THAT** WOULDA BEEN PRODUCTIVE!

BE THAT AS IT MAY, I'M AFRAID THE ODDS OF FINDING MY HAT IN THIS MESS ARE RAPIDLY **DWINDLING**!

LET'S GIVE IT ONE MORE TRY AROUND THE NEXT CORNER!

WHAT WE'VE GOT TO— **GREAT HEAPING YOICKS! THIS** YOU AIN'T GONNA BELIEVE!

WELL NOT QUITE! FOR THAT NIGHT FATE HAD ONE LAST CARD TO PLAY!

OBOY! OBOY! OBOY! DO IT! **OPEN** THAT BABY!

LET'S SEE...**12** TO THE RIGHT... ..**18** TO THE—

WHOOSH BANG

DING DING DING DING DING

NOW WHAT?

THE **WIND!** IT BLEW OPEN THE BALCONY DOORS AND TRIGGERED THE **UPSTAIRS** ALARM!

WHICH IS OUR CUE TO EXIT STAGE RIGHT, AND DON'T SPARE THE SHOE LEATHER!

BUT THE **JEWELS!**

THEY'LL DO US NO GOOD IN THE NICK, DIPPY! NOW **COME ON!**

AND SO—

BOY! THAT WAS SOME STORM LAST NIGHT!

YEAH, AND ACCORDING TO THIS, IT SEEMS TO HAVE FOILED A ROBBERY AT THE GILTBUNDLE ESTATE!

REALLY? DID THE POLICE CATCH THE BAD GUYS?

NOPE! LIKE THE HATS OF YESTERDAY...

...THEY WERE GONE WITH THE WIND!

DAILY BL